THE JOKE MACHINE

DISCLAIMER: READING THIS BOOK MAY CAUSE INTENSE LAUGHTER

The author, illustrator, and publisher of this book are not responsible for any uncontrollable giggling, guffawing, hipping, hooting, and hollering that may lead to sides splitting and bellies jiggling.

It's also possible that you could laugh your head off. Should that occur, please do not call us—not that you even could call in that condition, but please don't try. Go to the hospital instead.

Furthermore, we tried to keep the level of corniness to a minimum, but apparently the dog in our office has learned to type, and he has a very silly sense of humor. We thought we'd mention the dog here, since no one reads disclaimers anyway. Which leads us to ask: Why are you still reading this? Turn the page and learn how to be funny!

THE JOKE MACHINE

Create Your Own Jokes and
Become Instantly Funny!

*WRITTEN IN PEN,
BECAUSE SHE LIVES DANGEROUSLY,*
by **THERESA JULIAN**

*ILLUSTRATED, USING ONLY HIS TOES
AND A LITTLE ELBOW ACTION,*
by **PAT LEWIS**

Odd Dot **New York**

TO MARIA, NICK, DANA ROSE, AND DANIEL,
WHO ARE MY INSPIRATION AND JOY.
I LOVE YOU TO THE MOON AND BACK
—T.J.

TO PIXIE, THE BEST STUDIO CAT
—P.L.

Odd Dot

An imprint of Macmillan Publishing Group, LLC
120 Broadway, New York, NY 10271
OddDot.com

Text copyright © 2019 by Theresa Julian

Illustrations copyright © 2019 by Pat Lewis

Library of Congress Cataloging-in-Publication Data
is available.

ISBN: 978-1-250-31864-0

COVER DESIGNERS Colleen AF Venable and Tim Hall
INTERIOR DESIGNER Tim Hall
EDITOR Justin Krasner

Our books may be purchased in bulk for promotional,
educational, or business use. Please contact your local
bookseller or the Macmillan Corporate and Premium
Sales Department at (800) 221-7945 ext. 5442 or by email
at MacmillanSpecialMarkets@macmillan.com.

Printed in the United States of America by LSC
Communications, Crawfordsville, Indiana

First edition, 2019

1 3 5 7 9 10 8 6 4 2

CAUTION!

This Book Is So Blindingly Amazing Safety Glasses Are Required Beyond This Point

The Steps to
BEING FUNNY

THE FORMULA FOR FUNNY

Welcome to the Laugh Lab, a revolutionary facility that teaches you how to be funny! Here we build jokes, punch up puns, mash up words, and always wear silly hats.

Come on in! Don't be shy. We're just going to tickle your ribs, rattle your funny bone, and, okay, maybe ruffle your hair a little—but you could use a new look.

Here at the Laugh Lab, we believe that making people laugh is like a magic trick—a verbal magic trick. It's leading a thought one way, then—***surprise!***—you flip it in a different direction. It's like a magician distracting you with one hand so he can pull a chimichanga out of his pocket with the other.

1

Surprise is the key to making people laugh, but there's lots of other stuff that goes into it, too, like contrast, exaggeration, specifics, whoopee cushions, and bologna in your shoes. The thing is, with practice, *anyone* can be funny.

What's that? You want to get started? No problem!

We hired the world's top brainiacs to create a scientific formula that will make you instantly funnier:

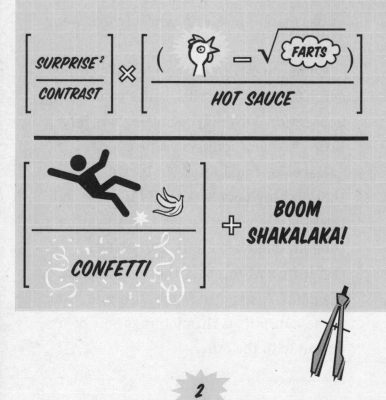

Does that formula really work? The answer is **NO!** Of course not! We made it up. We just wanted to make you laugh.

If you want to be funnier, turn the page and start your tour of the Laugh Lab. You'll learn a new funny-forming strategy in each room, which will help you create your own jokes and send your friends rolling in the aisles.*

— Your Friends at the Laugh Lab

* Not literally rolling, because that would cause broken bones and head trauma, but you know what we mean.

SURPRISE: DANGEROUS WORDS

Step aside! The master has arrived!

I'm Dr. Crankshaw, inventor of this scientific marvel—the joke machine! Yes, a machine that *builds jokes*. All you have to do is drop a few words into the whoozy-whatzy, mix in punctuation, confetti, an orange sock, flour and water, and—voilà—you have a fully formed joke.

Lovely, isn't she? I call her *LOLA*, which stands for *Laugh Out Loud Apparatus*.

No! Don't ask how *LOLA* works; she's so advanced she boggles the mind.

Just know that *LOLA* is a complex web of steel, plastic, and

electronics—all held together by marshmallow taffy.

This crackerjack of a machine has taught us that the key to humor is surprise. It's distracting someone with one thought, then—*boom!*—ending with something totally unexpected. It's the quick twist at the end that surprises us and makes us laugh.

Now, are you ready for **LOLA**? Excellent. Stand back while she creates a joke!

Don't mess with me, I know karate, judo, jujitsu, kung fu, and 20 other dangerous words.

Aha! **LOLA** used *surprise* to create a funny one-liner. The beginning of the sentence warns us not to mess with someone who knows martial arts. The end of the sentence surprises us, because we realize that the person doesn't know any martial arts, only the *words*.

Surprise is key to creating a good joke, but there's lots more to learn here at the lab. Stick with **LOLA**, and your laugh-making ability, as determined by our **Ha-Ha Meter**, will go from Total Snoozer to Super Sidesplitter!

HA-HA METER

SUPER SIDESPLITTER
BACKSLAPPER
BELLY BUSTER
SNICKLER
SNACKLER
CORNBALL
HUH?
TOTAL SNOOZER

YOUR TURN!

Now, the part that's more fun than dropping Pop Rocks into soda pop. **LOLA** will show you how to build your own jokes using surprise!

We create surprise with the **Vanilla Fruit Punch** method. The scientists here at the Laugh Lab developed this method using only a vanilla bean, a bag of fruit, some sugar, and a broken Scrabble game.

First, say a plain-vanilla fact. Then follow it up with a fruit punch—something that's totally unexpected.

Let's try it! Start with a vanilla sentence, such as:

> I like to exercise.

Now, add a surprising ending:

> I take long walks to the fridge.

Do you see what we just did? We fruit-punched it up!

Here are other examples of how to punch up your vanillas:

Vanilla Fruit Punch

My basketball team is really good at dunking.

Until we run out of cookies.

I don't really dance.

I more wiggle like a worm on a hot driveway.

Look at that huge spider!

It's like a guinea pig with eight legs!

Lunch today was pretty lousy.

I spent it in detention, chewing on erasers.

That dog isn't very bright.

I've met smarter stuffed animals.

When you use **Vanilla Fruit Punch**, ask yourself: What is the least likely way this thought should end? If you can come up with something that's surprising but still fits, you're on your way to Giggle Town. So go for it! Take those plain-vanilla words and turn them into a hot fudge sundae, with extra whipped cream, rainbow sprinkles, and lots of *nuts*!

Here are some jokes that use surprise. Share them with your friends!

SHIRTS AND SHOES ARE REQUIRED TO ENTER. PANTS MAY COME AND GO AS THEY PLEASE.

Do you know what's odd?
Every other number.

If history repeats itself . . . I am so getting a dinosaur.

Knock, knock.
Who's there?
Dwayne.
Dwayne who?
Dwayne the bathtub, I'm dwowning!

What do you call the soft tissue between a shark's teeth?

A slow swimmer.

Did you just pick your nose?

Nope. I was born with it.

We'll be best friends forever.
You already know too much.

Knock, knock.

Who's there?

Alex.

Alex who?

Alex the questions around here!

Teacher: If you have five dollars and ask your brother for another five, how many dollars would you have?

Student: Zero dollars.

Teacher: You don't know math.

Student: You don't know my brother.

You ate my potato chips?! What kind of a person are you?

Like you, only not hungry.

Music is so powerful it can transport you from one place to another. When my parents play polka in one room, I go hide in another.

Since you're eating healthy, I've removed all the junk food from the house. It was delicious.

The jokes I told at the birthday party had everyone crying with laughter— even the cake was in tiers.

Whoever said "nothing is impossible" never tried to get a mirror to stay up in her locker.

A spider wandered into my room last night, so I sat down and talked to him. Turns out he's a cool guy. He wants to be a web developer.

Our Brownie leader was really happy with how our glitter pictures were coming along, until someone turned on the fan.

Last night Grandpa was mad because he couldn't figure out how to work his iPad, and his resident tech specialist was sleeping. My cousin's five, and it was *WAY* past his bedtime.

I panicked because I thought there was a real emergency at the hardware store. Then I realized it was just a guy running around with a wrench in his hand, yelling, "This is not a drill!"

On our street, there's a "Watch for Children" sign. I keep taking my brother there, but still no watch.

The butcher invited my family to his house for a BBQ. When we got there, he pointed to his wife and said, "Meet Patty."

13

I USED TO FINGER PAINT IN MY PAJAMAS. NOW MOM SAYS I HAVE TO DO IT ON PAPER.

Why do fish live in salt water?
Because pepper makes them sneeze.

You know that feeling you get when you ace your math test? Yeah, neither do I.

I love u.
Really?
It's my favorite vowel.

> You don't have to be crazy to be my friend. I'll train you.

Dad: I'm going to wash the car with our son.
Mom: Can't you just use a sponge?

A Spanish magician told everyone he would disappear. He said, "Uno, dos . . ." and then disappeared without a tres.

Now button up your lab coat and blast off to the next room. More jokes await!

CONTRAST:
SOUP AND PICKLES

Dude! Ride on in here. I've got stuff to explain.

Don't look so surprised to see me. This room is about contrast. Apparently, I contrast with the scientist dude in the other room, so they hired me. They took one look at the taco stain on my shirt and said I was perfect.

Contrast is the *difference* between things. It's funny when things that are totally different are stuck together. It's like when you wear a fancy suit with flip-flops, your cat gnaws on your dog's bone, or your friend eats soup and pickles. What's with that?

15

Now I'm gonna drop a bunch of random stuff into this thing that looks like a rusty trash bin, and **LOLA** will . . .

What's the difference between a piano and a fish? **You can tune a piano, but you can't tuna fish!**

Tubular! **LOLA** spit out a joke that uses contrast. The question asks for the difference between a piano and a fish, and the answer contrasts *tune a piano* and *tuna fish*, two things that seemingly have nothing in common but sound alike. When we try to connect these two different things, we're surprised by the contrast and we laugh.

And, dude, here's the thing: When you use contrast, make sure the things you're contrasting are different but they kind of go together, too. If they're too crazy, the joke won't work.

Ready for another go? Joke me, *LOLA*!

What did
the green grape say
to the purple grape?
Breathe! Just breathe!

HA! In this joke, the fruits are contrasting colors—green and purple—but the cool thing is, they're both grapes, so they're alike, too. Plus, grapes and breathing don't usually go together so—totally unexpected and silly, dude!

Get amped—we're going to build some epic jokes using contrast.

Start with a person or thing. Then contrast that person or thing with something unexpected, to create surprise. Check out the totally sick jokes I stirred up:

Expected **UNEXPECTED, with CONTRAST**

I'm uncoordinated. I can't kick a ball.

I'm uncoordinated. I twist my ankle playing cards.

It's creepy when villains say mean things.

It's creepy when villains quote Shakespeare.

Superheroes zip around the world fighting crime and upholding justice.

Superheroes bowl free on Tuesdays if they help set up the pins and sweep the floors.

I'm worried when the groundhog says there's six more weeks of winter.

I'm worried when a groundhog talks.

I think I'll wear a skeleton costume on Halloween.

I think I'll wear a skeleton costume on this beautiful summer day so I can wander around the supermarket and squeeze lemons.

Lemons

Mrs. Rosewood is in class grading our English papers.

Mrs. Rosewood is suiting up to start a gig as a professional wrestler.

Time is precious. I need to use it wisely.

Time is precious. I need to waste it wisely.

Maria smiled at me. I smiled back.

Maria smiled at me. Now I don't have to lie to my journal.

My morning routine includes 20 repetitions on each of the 30 machines at the gym.

My morning routine includes 20 repetitions of hitting the snooze button on my alarm clock.

A balanced diet means the appropriate number of servings from each of the food groups.

A balanced diet means a cupcake in each hand.

20

Quantum physics is confusing.

Quantum physics is easy. What's confusing is a square box, a round pizza, and triangular slices.

Got it? Wild! Now dive into these jokes:

What's the difference between drinking three sodas and going to the bathroom?
About 20 minutes.

Why did the rooster cross the road?
To show everyone he wasn't a chicken.

What's the difference between a dinosaur that's sleeping and a dinosaur that won the lottery?
One is a dino-snore, and the other is a dino-score!

21

What's the difference between a
baseball player and a bad skydiver?
**The baseball player goes WHACK,
and the bad skydiver goes—Uh-oh . . .
WHACK!**

What's the difference between a fly
and Superman?
**Superman can fly, but a fly can't
superman.**

I was shopping for a new toilet but
couldn't decide if I wanted to buy it.
I figured I needed to sleep on it.

What's the difference between a
cornfield and a potato field?
**One has ears but can't hear, the other
has eyes but can't see.**

Teacher: What was the lesson from that novel?
Student: Don't read it.

How come **"you're a peach"** is a compliment but **"you're bananas"** is an insult?

Even though I trust my dog with my life, **I don't trust him with my hot dog.**

You're loud, annoying, and crazy, **which of course means we're going to be best friends.**

What's the difference between roast beef and pea soup?
Anyone can roast beef.

We're best friends. If you fall, I'll pick you up. **After I stop laughing.**

How are "dad" jokes and "little brother" jokes different?
In dad jokes, the punchline's a parent. In little brother jokes, nothing's funny.

What's the difference between a man who's wearing jeans and riding a bike, and a man who's wearing a tux and riding a unicycle?
Attire.

Did you know the human body is made up of nitrogen (**N**), carbon (**C**), hydrogen (**H**), and oxygen (**O**)? Basically we're one big **NaCHO**.

The kids I babysat for didn't listen to me. They wouldn't stop screaming and throwing pizza at each other. They even tied my hair to the fridge.
Whoa! They were bad kids?
No, perfectly normal.

My best friend and I lived happily for 11 years. **And then we met.**

Outside of a dog, a book is man's best friend. **Inside of a dog is a dark place.**

Get some air, and angle toward the next room!

COMPARISON:
COUGHING UP A CAT

Grrreetings! Sherlock Bones here, ready to dig deeper into this silly-osophy. I've been investigating joke making with the perseverance of a bulldog, and, well, I *am* a bulldog, so I've uncovered some **grrripping** stuff. I've found that using comparison is a bullish way to make your friends laugh.

Comparison is finding the *similarity* between things. When making a joke, you can use comparison to describe one thing by associating it with another thing.

When we point out a similarity between two random things, we're surprised and we laugh. Using comparison is as much fun as barking at pigeons, chasing your tail, or waiting for the fridge door to open.

Toss us a joke, *LOLA*, and make sure it's about the **grrreatest** species on the planet!

I happen to think that joke machines are the best species on the planet, but I know you want a dog joke, so here goes: Is that a Chihuahua on the couch, or a snoring cannoli?

Woof! LOLA's comparing a sleeping Chihuahua with a snoring dessert. Those are as different as sugar and sriracha—but weirdly—they're alike, too. They're both small, long, and brown—like me, and also like . . . uh . . . never mind! When we realize the similarity between these two different things, we're caught off guard and we laugh.

LOLA, another joke. And make sure it's not a cat joke!

Adjust your cat-titude, Sherlock! I happen to think cats are the cream doughnuts of the animal world, so . . .

How is a cat like a coin? **It has a head on one side and a tail on the other.**

Grrross! That joke's a cat-astrophe . . . *But* it is a good example of a comparison that uses the word *like*. Many comparison jokes are similes, which show how one thing is like another. They point out the connection between two different things—such as a cat and a coin—and we giggle at the similarity.

Now I need to paws this convo. My brain is allergic to cats, and all this talk is making me *sneeze*!

How is a cat like a coin?
It has a head on one side and a tail on the other.

What Are Similes and Metaphors?

A **simile** compares things using the word *like* or *as*:

My locker is like the Bermuda Triangle. Stuff goes in and never comes out.

A **metaphor** directly states a comparison:

You are the peanut butter to my jelly.

Grrreat, a cat-free page! A perfect place to show you how to brainstorm your own jokes using comparison. Brainstorming is writing fast and not worrying about whether it's good or a smelly pile of dog poop. Just write whatever pops into your head. Then, sift through the random ideas, figure out which work, and put them together like the pieces of a puzzle.

Quick! Throw out a topic.

Peanut butter? Doggone great! Let's brainstorm about peanut butter. Shout out things you could compare peanut butter to for the first few letters of the alphabet. Here are some ideas:

> **A.** alligator drool
>
> **B.** butt sweat
>
> **C.** cotton candy
>
> **D.** dried donkey boogers
>
> **E.** earwax
>
> **F.** a Frisbee
>
> **G.** grape soda
>
> **H.** hand lotion

Now I'm going to do something my obedience school teacher wouldn't approve of. Mrs. Pecan, if you're reading this, close your eyes!

What brand of peanut butter is this? It tastes like butt sweat.

How old is this peanut butter sandwich? It's as hard as a Frisbee.

Whoa! This peanut butter is so creamy, it's like eating hand lotion.

Did you get this peanut butter from the medicine cabinet? It tastes like earwax.

This peanut butter's extra crunchy. What's in here, dried donkey boogers?

Got it? Now clean the peanut butter off your face, don't forget the glob on your shoe, and dig into these jokes!

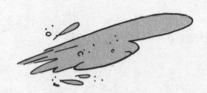

School is like a walk in the park . . .
Jurassic Park!

How is a baseball team like a muffin?
They both depend on the batter.

How do you know your toothbrush is getting old?
It's as furry as a moldy pickle.

How are false teeth like stars?
They come out at night.

Are you walking a Great Dane or a horse that can bark?

What do music and chickens have in common?
Bach, Bach, Bach!

Her smile was like a witch's, right before she pushes you into her bubbling cauldron.

What's smarter than a talking bird?
A spelling bee.

After running, his breath sounded like Darth Vader's.

Stay away from the cookies. We're not supposed to eat them now.
I'm just smelling them. It's like eating with your nose.

Walking to school is hard. It's like climbing Mount Everest in flip-flops.

Don't trust her. She's as slippery as a banana peel.

The cafeteria went crazy when the class moms brought out the chocolate-covered caramel bars. It was more like *The Hunger Games* **than a** *Welcome-to-Sixth-Grade Lunch Party.*

Starting at a new school felt weird, like when you're on vacation in another state and all the TV channels are different.

How are doughnuts and golf alike?
They both have a hole in one.

Who's richer—the butcher, the baker, or the candlestick maker?
The baker, because he has lots of dough.

He's slowly growing on me, like bacteria in a petri dish.

Which runs faster, hot or cold water?
Hot, because you can catch cold.

My thesaurus is terrible. It's also terrible.

I was really scared on the roller coaster, and trust me, I don't scare easily. I've eaten the beans in the school cafeteria.

Yowza! What's in this sandwich? It tastes like old worms in a bun.

Terrific! Now scamper to the next page!

EXAGGERATION:
49 GUMMIES

Hey! I'm Captain 'Mazing. I'm really good at *everything*. I'm supersmart and incredibly fast, I have ginormous muscles, and I'm the only kid on the block who can fit 49 gummies in his mouth. Oh, and my macaroni art—kills it, right?

For some reason, the scientists here want me to talk about exaggeration, which means **STRETCHING** the truth. It's like my saying I built this macaroni skyscraper in 30 seconds, which is an exaggeration, because it took me 40 seconds. Max.

Okay, *LOLA*, tell us a joke about the *coolest* person on the planet, which—no joke—is me.

Awesome Stuff

WHOOZY-WHATZY
pat. pending

Science called. It wants to borrow some of your macaroni to fill up the black holes in outer space.

What?! *LOLA*'s exaggerating. I don't have enough macaroni to fill up *all* the black holes. Only most of them. *Jeez*, *LOLA*, too bad you're not as smart as I am.

Gggreep. Gggrupp. Tttsaap. Zzzoop. YAPPP!

Huh? **LOLA**, what are you saying?

I'm the smart one!

I'm so smart Google texts me when it's got nothing!

I'm so smart the future calls me to find out what it should do next.

I'm so smart libraries across the country are renaming themselves after me. The librarians, too!

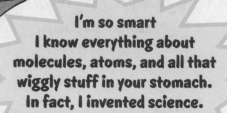

I'm so smart
I know everything about
molecules, atoms, and all that
wiggly stuff in your stomach.
In fact, I invented science.

I'm so smart
that when I talk,
people raise their
eyebrows so high they
touch their scalps.

I'm so smart the
dictionary is now only a
single page that says
Want to know stuff? Call
LOLA at 555-275-5652.

Tater tots! **LOLA** thinks she's smarter
than I am? She's on overload and ready to
explode! Quick—hop into my Lego spaceship, and I'll fly you to the next page.

YOUR TURN!

Want to know how to create jokes that use exaggeration? Start with something ordinary, like a gummy worm, and pull one part of it so it's superdistorted and silly but still looks like a worm. Exaggerate so it's funny but also makes sense. It can't be so loopy that it's complete bonkers.

Now try this:

1. **Pick something interesting to talk about—like ME!**

2. **Laser-beam in on one thing about your topic—like how fast I am.**

3. **Make a list of action verbs— in this case, things that can be done fast—like:**

RUN   WRITE
SWIM   KICK
DRAW   BRUSH
EAT   SMILE
TALK   THINK
DANCE   PAINT
COOK   READ
LAUGH   SING
TYPE   GROW
HOP   BURP
MOVE   SLEEP
JUMP   GROAN

Now use some of these words to describe my doing something fast, and exaggerate how fast (which is impossible, because I'm supersonic, but go ahead and *try*). Pretend it's a puzzle, and keep working it until something fits and it's funny. Here are some incredible examples:

I ran around the track so fast I started and finished in the same second.

I typed my history essay so fast I wore off my fingerprints.

I'm so fast I burp *before* I drink soda.

My hair grows so fast I trim it every five minutes.

I'm not sad. I smiled so fast you missed it.

Yes, I was dancing. I was just so fast you couldn't see my sweet moves.

I draw so fast my crayons spark.

Don't slow down! Charge into these jokes:

Knock, knock.
Who's there?
Pasture.
Pasture who?
It's so far pasture bedtime on Tuesday it's already time for lunch on Wednesday.

It's so cold I saw polar bears wearing hats and jackets.

On the first day of school I had so much adrenaline pumping through my body, if I channeled it, I could have powered seven rides at Six Flags.

Studying means 10 percent reading and 90 percent complaining to your friends that you have to study.

30 days has September, April, June, and November. All the rest have 31 except January, which has 6,952.

I live in the sunny part of Washington. It only rains from May to May.

I was always smart, even as a baby.
What did you used to do?
Change my own diaper, make my own baby food, and drive myself to play dates. I basically raised myself.

Why did you take advice from that guy? His brain is smaller than half a raisin.

I'm so hungry I could eat my feet.

Knock, knock!
Who's there?
Ben.
Ben who?
Ben knockin' on the door all afternoon.

Our science teacher is so boring, the periodic table is starting to remind me of my patchwork quilt.

All my little brother does is buy toys. Once, he was bedridden for a week, and Lego almost went under!

I've told you a million times to stop exaggerating.

He was swimming so fast the lifeguard gave him a speeding ticket.

What animal has more lives than a cat?
Frogs, they croak millions of times.

I walked so far my feet sent me a text that said, "Tomorrow walk on your hands."

I drank so much water my nose started drizzling.

The sight was so ugly my eyeballs sent me a text that said, "Shut the lids!"

My mom is so old she still remembers how to use a semicolon.

My sister has so much hair she can hide anything in it: a comb, a brush, her homework, a puppy.

What type of thief can lift five million pounds?
A shoplifter.

Knock, knock.
Who's there?
120.
120 who?
120 percent chance you won't get this joke.

I'm so broke I can't even pay attention.

The beef in my burger is so rare, it's starting to eat the lettuce.

Those were obviously the best jokes in the universe, right? Keep reading for more amazing stuff!

UNDERSTATEMENT:
THE CORN MUFFIN OF JOKES

Shh! Come in quietly. **LOLA**'s a bit ruffled. That bean-headed kid in the last room upset her—him and all his exaggeration. I'm making a raspberry soufflé to cheer her up. Too much noise, and my soufflé will collapse, so I have to whisper.

This room is about understatement, another way to make your friends laugh. Understatement is the opposite of exaggeration. It's saying something with less emphasis than it deserves. Understating is a laid-back, dry humor—which means saying something funny but pretending it's serious. Understatement is kind of like the corn muffin of jokes. The flourless cake. The doughnut with no sprinkles. So let's . . .

Oh dear.

Hmm. I might need a bigger cup.

Since **LOLA**'s resting, I'll just tell you about understatement. It's like a car chase in a movie with *really* slow-moving cars—it's funny because it's not logical; it's the opposite of what we think should happen.

When you use understatement, speak in a casual, monotone voice. If you lower your tone, speak slower, and dish out the punch line with a completely straight face, the words are even funnier. It's like talking in all lower case. Skip the exclamation points, too.

Hmm. Would you look at those flames? I guess we better mosey on to the next page.

YOUR TURN!

Lovely. This page is much cooler.

So how can you use understatement to cook up your own jokes? Start with a list of situations, and create responses that have less emotion or urgency than they deserve. Instead of addressing the problem, really stir it up by purposefully missing the point. Comment on something offbeat about the situation.

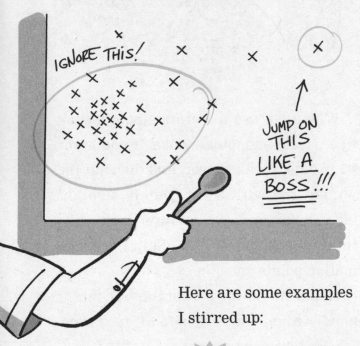

Here are some examples I stirred up:

50

Situation **UNDERSTATED RESPONSE**

You step on your friend's toe. You think it's broken.

It's okay. You really only need eight toes, seven, tops.

The roof has blown off your restaurant.

We're still open for business. We're just more open than usual.

You are in a haunted house, and a green monster is chasing you. You fall down a flight of stairs, bang your arm, and twist your shoulder.

There's nothing to worry about. I'm fine. And by the way, do you know how to get to the hospital?

Aliens land on Earth, and your friend is trying to hide.

Don't worry. They're looking for brains. You're safe.

51

Your friend falls off his bike and cracks a tooth.

Whoa, your hair's getting long. You need a haircut.

Everyone brought elaborate, carefully prepared dishes to the barbecue.

Here's my contribution—my famous family recipe for "bag of ice."

You owe your friend $120 for a bike, $95 for a video game, and $360 for magic seeds—the ones that were supposed to grow into your dream car.

Dude, I picked the wrong week to give up my paper route.

Someone thinks you've created an amazing piece of art. They love the colors, the texture, the swirls!

Er, it's just a cupcake that fell on paper and got licked by my iguana.

It's Art... Gecko?

Now ease on into these jokes:

There are so many policemen at this baseball game. Something must be wrong.
I bet someone stole a base.

I was walking down an alley and came face-to-face with a really scary ghost!
What did you do?
Nothing. I could see right through him.

I just fell off a 30-foot ladder!
Are you okay?
Yeah, I was on the first step.

Old Man: You said you'd spend your whole life trying to make me happy.
Old Woman: I didn't expect to live this long.

I was in the bank, and a masked gunman ran in and shouted at me:
"You're the one who I want to rob!"
I was so upset. I couldn't believe he didn't know it's "You're the one *whom* I want to rob."

Patient: My back hurts when I wake up in the morning.
Doctor: Then get up in the afternoon.

What do you call a guy with a rubber toe?
Roberto.

Back in the day, I walked 10 miles to the store and carried my groceries back in all kinds of weather. So yeah, online shopping with two-hour delivery is a *little* more convenient.

Doctor, doctor, I keep seeing a gigantic insect march across the room going *boom, boom, boom.*
Don't worry; it's just a bug that's going around.

A 500-pound grizzly wandered into our garage and roared. He had giant claws, razor-sharp teeth, and powerful arms, but mostly I was surprised that he wasn't wearing socks. Completely bear feet.

You sleepwalk
every night.
Doesn't that
scare you?
**No, I'm living
the dream.**

I spent all weekend reading about how
you should eat more vegetables, get
more sleep, and exercise more. So I
stopped reading.

Doctor, doctor, I'm going to die in 59
seconds!
I'll be with you in a minute.

**It's so terrible; my neighbor just died
and was buried in the wrong hole. It
was a grave mistake.**

Help! Stop that rhino from charging.
Just take away its credit card.

Two people died yesterday when strong
winds blew down a lemon tree.
It was a bitter blow.

All the eighth-grade art projects were accidentally thrown into the garbage. It was a great tragedy in the world of art, more than just the misuse of pipe cleaners and cotton balls that we're used to.

I lost my new iPhone! Oh no!
Don't worry; my science teacher said the universe is infinite. It's here somewhere.

What happens when a red ship crashes into a blue ship?
The crew gets marooned.

Something's wrong. I keep picturing myself as a bridge.
What's come over you?
Two cars, a truck, and a bus.

Can you give me something for a headache?
Stare at these mind games for three hours, you'll have a headache.

Look at that troll! His ears are as big as toasters!

I'd say they're "noticeable."

Patient: Help! I broke my arm in two places.

Doctor: Then stop going to those places.

Help! There's a kidnapping in the park.

Just wake him up.

I'm such a fast thinker I'm going to answer your question *before* you ask it.

Goodness. One of the jokes from the Exaggeration Room has leaked into the Understatement Room. Hold your nose while I fumigate. I need to cover every inch of this room with highly toxic spray . . .

Now I'll get back to my tea. You need to skedaddle to the next room. Oh, and bring a spoon so you can scoop out some more silliness.

What Is Sarcasm?

Sarcasm is saying the opposite of what you mean, saying something to make another person feel stupid, or saying something to show that you're angry. An example is saying a snarky "That's great" when you really mean "That's lame." We at the Laugh Lab suggest you steer clear of sarcasm. It can be hurtful, and it's hard to pull off when writing or texting, because it relies on a snippy tone. Instead, be a respectful jokester! Stay jolly and positive. We suggest you don't slump in the swamps of sarcasm but soar on the wings of wit!

SPECIFICS:
BUNNY-PRINT JAMMIES

Enough!

These shenanigans have to stop. From this page forward, there'll be no more fire starting, macaroni arting, fumigating, or any other foofarawing in this facility! **LOLA** is a sophisticated piece of equipment designed by brilliant scientists—the kind who carry protractors and wear pencils behind their ears. I can't have goopy macaroni and sticky fumes gumming up the works!

LOLA's back up and humming and ready to create jokes about specifics, another key to making your friends laugh. Specifics are details that describe something just right. Instead of saying something ordinary, like "**LOLA** would look great in a hat," I can use some juicy specifics and say "**LOLA** would look great in a polka-dotted beanie with a propeller that goes *weeeeeeee woooo* in the wind."

I can say, "Every night, **LOLA** puts on her jammies," or I can say, "Every night, **LOLA** puts on fuzzy bunny-print jammies, the kind with the plastic feet that go *schleep, schleep, schleep* across the floor." See how specifics can be spiffalicious?

LOLA, show us what you have!

 Okay, Dr. Crankshaw, you asked for it. Here are some specifics:

LOLA'S NEW LAUGH LAB RULES
(IN ADDITION TO NO FIRE STARTING OR FUMIGATING)

RULE #1: The surfer dude cannot fill the floor with sand for his beach parties. My air vents have sucked in so much sand they look like they're lined with crumb cake.

Ah! Good use of specifics: "air vents lined with crumb cake!"

RULE #2: Sherlock Bones cannot run to the door every time he hears a knock-knock joke. I've told him 2,907 times, no one's at the door! He needs to lift up those long, scraggly jelly ears and listen to what I'm saying!

Excellent! More specifics: "2,907 times" and "long, scraggly jelly ears."

RULE #3: Dr. Crankshaw needs to stop using highfalutin, hippity-dippity words. All his mad-scientist mumbo jumbo is making my wires loopy.

First, great use of specifics by referring to my words as "highfalutin" and "hippity-dippity."

Second, I'm not a mad scientist! Maybe a little cranky, but definitely not mad! Do mad scientists say "how-de-do" with a cheery smile, as I do? Do mad scientists share their caramel corn at lunch? Do mad scientists separate plastic, metal, and glass for recycling?!

I think **LOLA** needs another adjustment.

While **LOLA**'s, uh, resting, let's spiff up some sentences with specifics. Make your friends laugh by describing things with unexpected details. Really fancy-schmancy it up, and pick specifics that paint a picture or make us smell, feel, or otherwise sense something. But wait! Also make sure the specifics fit the situation. If they don't fit, it's just a discombobulated heap of humbuggery.

Start with an ordinary sentence, and brainstorm until you hit on something funny, like this:

Ordinary: My shoes smell bad.

With Specifics: My shoes smell like the bottom of an old lady's purse.

My shoes smell like I scooped them out of the litter box.

My shoes smell like they've been in my gym locker since second grade.

My shoes smell like my dog's squeaky toy.

My shoes smell like bug spray. The cheap kind.

Ordinary: I can't believe I spilled food on my shirt.

With Specifics: I look like a vat of chili exploded on me.

I look like a dish of spaghetti died on me.

I look like I fell in that bucket of gray water the custodian uses to wash the cafeteria floor.

I look like a bunch of two-year-olds had a Play-Doh party on my shirt.

I look like a caveman who washes his clothes in a muddy river and beats them with a rock.

Now jump into more jokes that use specifics!

This zucchini is as soggy as the frog guts I dissected in science lab yesterday.

When you slurp your spaghetti, you sound like the toilet that hiccups in the girls' bathroom.

What's black and white and makes a lot of noise?
A zebra jumping on Bubble Wrap.

You have so many eraser holes in your worksheet it looks like the surface of the moon.

The rain is making my hair curl up like Cheetos.

There are so many things stuck between my teeth it seems as if I'm brushing them with glue.

There are so many broken crayons in here they look like a box of jelly beans.

I'm so confused! My head is spinning like an astronaut in zero gravity.

When my feet touched the bottom of the mucky river, it felt as though my toes were sinking into cherry pie.

Your outfit has so many stripes you look like a zebra wearing striped socks, eating a Pixy Stix.

I'm tired and upset, and my brain is fried. Even my hair hurts.

That dog snarled at me as though he wanted to jump down my throat and suck out my intestines.

The train was dark, crowded, and smelled like my arm after I got the cast off.

Knock, knock.
Who's there?
Turning.
Turning who?
Turning into a poopie parrot pie face.

The history homework is confusing. Can you explain it?
No, to me it's as clear as frosted glass.

My friend got tired of my trying to make him laugh by putting a whoopee cushion on his chair. Now I fill the whoopee cushion with gravy and cheese.

What does a cat like to eat on a summer day?
A mice-cream cone.

68

What's the difference between a teacher and a train?
One goes "Spit out that gum" and the other goes "chew, chew."

I was so sick I threw up slime that looked like a river of creamed corn mixed with ham.

Knock, knock.
Who's there?
Lettuce.
Lettuce who?
Lettuce in; it's so cold out my eyelashes cracked off and my nose is dripping yellow icicles.

What is invisible and smells like carrots?
A rabbit fart.

Knock, knock.
Who's there?
I'm so.
I'm so who?
I'm so interested I could listen to you blab for an hour without blinking.

I stink at baseball. I'm not fast or limber, and I have short arms, like a T. rex.

How do you talk to a giant?
Use big words, like toilettenburstenbenutzungsanweisung.

I'm tired. I can't keep walking. I feel like a Lego man whose feet are stuck to that bumpy grid thing.

Oh, hello. Don't mind me. I'm just tightening some of **LOLA**'s screws. She has a few that are loose. But don't worry—I'll have her fixed before you can say, "Six thick thistle sticks."

BEING LITERAL:
A CUTE ANGLE

You recognize me, don't you? I'm your math teacher.

What's that? I don't look like your math teacher? Well, I am. I'm all the math teachers in the world rolled up into one very precise, fractionally correct person.

To me, math is the only subject that *counts*. All other subjects are like a circle—*pointless*. I think a really juicy math problem is what makes the world go 'round. Well, that and *earth's poles and gravity*.

That last sentence is an example of being literal. It states what *actually* makes the world go around. Speaking literally is ignoring what is meant and, instead, focusing on the exact words. Being literal is as funny as a square pizza because we're not expecting someone to

respond to our words; we're expecting them to respond to our meaning.

To help you, we math teachers put pencil to paper and created a numerically precise formula that will help you use literalness for laughs:

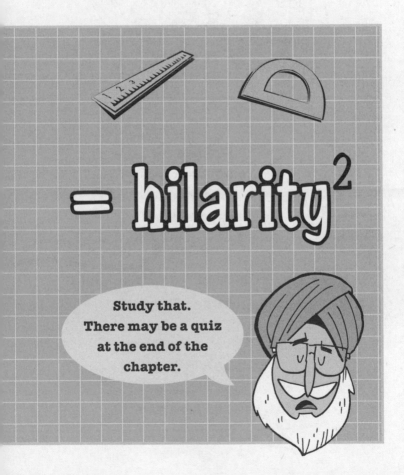

= hilarity²

Study that. There may be a quiz at the end of the chapter.

LOLA, give us an example of being literal, and make it mathy. Really mathy!

Why was the math book sad? It had too many problems.

Okay, fine—that joke was literal. But it could have been mathier. Try again!

Bobby bought 98 bicycles and sold 2. What does he have now? Debt.

Holy improper fraction! Are you making fun of word problems?

Dear Math, grow up and solve your own problems. I'm tired of solving them for you!

$$n = \sqrt{1 + \tfrac{3}{2}}\ (x + ab)^2$$

$$\Sigma = \tan X - \tfrac{8}{15}$$

$$e + \tfrac{1}{\sqrt{y}}$$

$$\times 1 . ! 2$$

$$10.3 \quad Y \quad \cos \frac{ab + c^2}{1}$$

The first step is to admit you have a problem.

I was good at math until they started adding the alphabet.

Parallel lines have a lot in common. Too bad they'll never meet.

What's odd to me are numbers that aren't divisible by two.

Why are circles so hot? They're 360 degrees.

Are you cold?
Come sit in the corner—
it's 90 degrees.

No one mocks math. Extra work for you, **LOLA**!

Due by three o'clock. Show your work!

YOUR TURN!

While **LOLA**'s doing her math homework, which will be all fun and games until she gets to the problem that divides by zero, let's create jokes by being literal.

If your friend asks a question or makes a statement, brainstorm a way to respond literally. Zero in on the *actual* words, not the *meaning* of the words, like this:

Friend: The restaurant looks crowded. Do you think there are any seats?
You: Dude, all restaurants have seats!

Friend: What do you make at your job?
You: Mostly mistakes.

Friend: I have so much work to do. I'm going home and hitting the books.
You: I suggest you open them and read them.

Friend: I'd bend over backward to get that after-school job.
You: It'd be easier to fill out an application.

Friend: You're doing multiplication on the floor?
You: Our teacher said we can't use tables.

Friend: I can't understand this homework. I just can't cut the mustard.
You: You can't cut ketchup or mayo, either.

Friend: Joe's a dead ringer for his brother.
You: He looks alive to me.

Friend: This assignment is so hard. Our teacher really wants a pound of flesh.
You: Yikes! I thought she wanted eight pages, double-spaced.

Friend: This fried chicken is terrible. I'm not a fan.
You: Correct, you're a person.

Friend: This Monopoly game is fun. Stand back—I'm going for broke!
You: I thought you were going for Park Place.

Friend: I'll go out on a limb and say you probably made the team.
You: No need to climb a tree. Soccer's played on the ground.

Friend: Why are chefs always so tough?
You: Because they *beat* eggs, *whip* cream, and *mash* potatoes.

Friend: Brad dropped his phone in the toilet. He got mad and lost his head.
You: He lost an $800 iPhone, too!

Now enjoy these jokes. No fractional laughs here—only full, whole-bodied hooting!

Can you name a car that starts with P?
No, they all start with gasoline.

80

What's the last thing that goes through
a bug's mind when it hits a windshield?
Its butt.

Why did the student eat his homework?
The teacher said it was a piece of cake.

**I finally found love! It's in the
dictionary, page 293. Bottom left.**

What do you call a fish with no eye?
Fsh.

Think of a number between 0 and 20.
Add 16 to it. Multiply by 2. Subtract 4.
Now close your eyes. It's dark, isn't it?

When is the best time to go shopping?
When the stores are open.

Yesterday someone asked me to donate to the local pool. I gave him a glass of water.

How do you make a fire with two sticks?
Make sure one's a match.

What's the best way to talk to a lion?
From a distance!

Do you know what will happen if we don't win?
We'll lose.

You're the meanest person on the planet.
Impossible. Do you know everyone on the planet?

What side of the turkey has the most feathers?
The outside.

Where were french fries first made?
France?
No, grease.

What do you call a zombie that writes music?
A decomposer.

Why did your dad put a clock under his desk?
Because he wanted to work overtime.

Trouble is my middle name! Well, actually, it's Jane.

What always comes at the end of Thanksgiving?
G!

What building has the most stories in any city?
The library.

What do you call a boomerang that doesn't work?
A stick.

If you threw your brown history book into the Red Sea, would it become red?
No, wet.

Why can't humans hear a dog whistle?
Because dogs can't whistle.

I was drinking chocolate milk in my slippers this morning, and I thought, "I really should wash some mugs."

Your shoes are on the wrong feet.
These are the only feet I have.

What do you call an old snowman?
Water.

Like pi, I could go on forever, but I won't. Time to slope off to the next page.

BUILDUP and TIMING: SUPERCHARGING THE BOOM

Put on a hard hat. You're entering the construction zone!

Also, just for the record, I'm the one who got the *LOLA*-meister up and humming two chapters back. That crazy Crankshaw was trying to tighten her screws with a banana. It took me three hours to clean banana mush out of her fuel injector.

Anyhoo, now that you know what makes something funny, let's build a joke, brick by brick.

Most jokes have a **setup**, a **buildup**, a **pause**, and a **payoff**. The setup introduces the subject. The buildup draws us in and drives the thought in a specific direction. The pause makes us anticipate what's coming. And the payoff, that's—*boom!*—the quick twist at the end.

LOLA! What are you building for us today?

Knock, knock.
Who's there?
Figs.
Figs who?
Figs the doorbell. It's broken!

LOLA's so funny! There's no way the doorbell's broken. That thing's more powerful than the 600-horsepower toaster I built yesterday. But notice how ***LOLA***'s joke has a four-part structure:

Setup: **Knock, knock.** *Who's there?*
Buildup: **Figs**. *Figs who?*
Pause.
Payoff: **Figs the doorbell. It's broken!**

Now you're probably wondering how long to pause. It's usually a second or two, just enough time to create anticipation. However, a long pause can be funny, too. A pause that's uncomfortably long is unexpected and silly.

To help you figure out how long to pause, I hammered out a high-powered pause formula. I'm going to whisper the formula, because if the math teacher hears, he'll charge in with his red pen and correct my equation. He might give me homework, too, so **shh**.

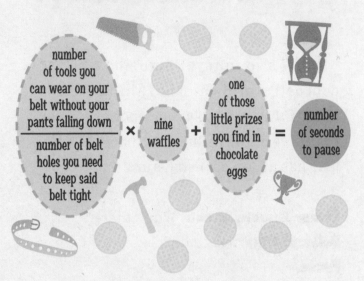

$$\frac{\text{number of tools you can wear on your belt without your pants falling down}}{\text{number of belt holes you need to keep said belt tight}} \times \text{nine waffles} + \text{one of those little prizes you find in chocolate eggs} = \text{number of seconds to pause}$$

After the pause—*bam!*—be confident and go straight for the *punch!*

YOUR TURN!

Time to accelerate and build your own jokes! For the record, here's what we're driving toward:

1. **Setup:** Introduce an idea that's based in reality. Set a tone. This part does not have to be funny.

2. **Buildup:** Tell us what's happening with increasing exaggeration. Create an attitude. Build anticipation. This part does not have to be funny.

3. **Pause:** Stop for dramatic effect.

4. **Payoff:** *Punch it!* **This part *has* to be funny.**

Want to create a joke using the four-part structure? Drive in reverse. Yes, write backward! First, find a funny punch line. Then think of how you can set it up.

Let's say you're eating lunch with friends. Start with a funny line like this:

This is the unhappiest I've been eating chocolate pudding.

Then create a setup and buildup, and don't forget the pause.

Setup: I had a terrible morning.

Buildup: I got a C on my English test, and we're starting decimals in math.

Pause.

Payoff: This is the unhappiest I've been eating chocolate pudding.

Here's another example:

You don't win friends with tuna.

Try to make your friends laugh by passing out cookies at lunch and saying this:

Setup: Everyone, have a cookie! I told my mom I wanted to bring a snack for my friends.

Buildup: She handed me a tuna sandwich, but I told her, "Mom, I need something good."

Pause.

Payoff: "You don't win friends with tuna."

Or start with this punch line:

How do I like my eggs? In a cake.

While you're at lunch, say:

Setup: This sandwich is really good.
Too bad no one else likes the kinds of
things I like.
   (Your friend will probably ask what you
like to eat.)
Buildup: I like my spaghetti with no
sauce. Burger with only mustard. And
my eggs...
Pause.
Payoff: In a cake.

Step on the pedal and drive into these
jokes!

If you can't remember my name / just
say chocolate / **I'll turn around**.

Student: Would you punish me for
something I didn't do? / **Teacher:** Of
course not. / **Student: Good, because I
didn't do my homework.**

I went to see the Liberty Bell. / I don't know why everyone makes such a big deal about it. / **It's not all it's cracked up to be.**

My teacher asked me to write a song about my life. / That made me nervous / **but then I composed myself.**

I walk around like everything is fine. / But deep down, inside my shoe, / **my sock is only half on.**

I eat cake every day. / Somewhere out there it's someone's birthday / **and I like to celebrate.**

I hope we can stay good friends until we die / Then I hope we can become ghost friends, / **walk through walls, and scare people.**

Roses are red, violets are blue, sunflowers are yellow. / I bet you were expecting something lovey-dovey, / **but no, these are just gardening facts.**

How many hyenas can fit in a car? Eight. / How many chickens can fit in a car? / **None, the car is already full of hyenas.**

Three friends, stranded on a desert island, find a magic lantern containing a genie. She grants them each a wish. / The first friend wishes he was back home. The second friend wishes the same. / **The third friend says, "I'm lonely. I wish my friends were back on this island."**

Don't eat Grandma. / Don't eat, Grandma. / **See how punctuation matters?**

Knock, knock. *Who's there?* / Nana. *Nana who?* / **Nana your business**.

Dear sleep, / I'm sorry we broke up this morning / **I want you back!**

I bought an environmentally friendly car. / It had a wooden body, wooden engine, and wooden seats. / **Only problem: It wooden go.**

Dance like no one's watching. / They're not. / **They're all checking their phones.**

When I was little, my mom used to make alphabet soup. / She said I loved it. / **I didn't; she was just putting words in my mouth.**

Exercise creates blood flow and helps you make decisions. / After going to the gym yesterday, I made a decision: / **I'm never going to the gym again.**

My dad's boss asked him to work on the weekend. / My dad said he'd come in but might be late because of traffic. His boss asked, "Okay, what time will you be in?" / **My dad said, "Monday."**

A lady asked me to fax her some papers. / I said I can't fax from where I live. The lady asked where I live. / **I told her "the present."**

Yesterday I tried on something from 5 years ago, and it still fits. / It was a scarf, but still, / **I'm trying to stay positive.**

95

Knock, knock. *Who's there?* / Boo. *Boo who?* / **Don't cry; it's only a joke.**

I walked into a library and asked for a book on turtles. / "Hardback?" the librarian asked. / **"Yes," I said, "with little legs."**

You know the drill! Speed on over to the next page.

FUNNY FOUNDATION:
EYE-POPPING STUFF

Catch that eyeball!

Schleep! There—it's back in. Good as new.

Oh, don't be squeamish. My eyeballs pop out so often I keep a jar of spares in the fridge—second shelf down, between the ketchup and mustard.

What? You think that's gross? I can't be running out for new eyeballs every five minutes. First, I'm a *painting*, and, second, it's illegal to drive without eyeballs.

Eyeballs bouncing across a page is a devilishly good example of starting with a funny foundation. To create humor, invent a silly situation—or, start with a real event and exaggerate what's happening. Then, use specifics and unexpected details to describe the action. Create a scene that's over-the-top, with lots of strong opinion.

The eye-opening part is this: The funnier the foundation, the easier it is to create jokes. A joke about your friend stubbing his toe may not be as funny as a joke about Dr. Crankshaw banging his toe on the couch and then doing a frenzied dance around the living room, out the door, and down a crowded street. A joke about your mom chaperoning your middle-school dance may not be as funny as a joke about Dr. Crankshaw chaperoning your middle-school dance and taking a whirl around the dance floor with your English teacher.

Eye-popping, right?

Okay, it's time. **LOLA**, let's *see* what you have!

What do you call a gorilla with bananas in his ears? Anything. He can't hear you.

Yes! A gorilla with bananas in his ears! Great place to start a joke.

Oh no! I swallowed an entire Scrabble game. My next trip to the bathroom could spell disaster.

Two pickles were fighting in a jar. What did one say to the other after pushing him out? Dill with it.

100

Bllleep!
There it
goes again!
I knew I shouldn't
have bought the
bargain eyeball glue.

YOUR TURN!

Time for you to create your own silly situations because I have to catch that peeper. When Dr. Crankshaw runs in here and gives me that "get-back-to-work" look, I need to be able to roll both eyeballs.

One way to create funny foundations is to use situational irony. With irony, there's a big difference between what we think will happen and what really does happen. It's like when the firehouse burns down or a TV weatherperson gets caught without an umbrella: the *opposite* of what we expect, right? To create a funny situation, list some nouns, and the *least likely* thing each would do.

Noun		Funny Situation

LeBron James...	...stinks at kickball.
A bus with a SAFETY FIRST sign...	...crashes into a building.
A police station...	...gets robbed.
Water Street...	...is a sandy street in the desert.
A social media quote...	...complains about how useless social media is.
A ferocious lion...	...is named Cupcake.

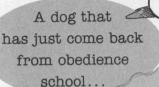

A dog that has just come back from obedience school...

...chews up his school certificate.

Posters about how to save paper...

...are posted everywhere.

The "Wind Seeker" ride at an amusement park...

...is closed due to high winds.

A pilot...

...is afraid of heights.

The procrastinator's meeting...

...is postponed.

The building of a roofing company . . . . . . has a roof that's caving in.

You go for dinner at Red Lobster . . . . . . except they're out of lobster.

A poster for the movie *Gravity* . . . . . . slips down.

A bottle of antichewing spray for dogs . . . . . . is all chewed up.

A tow truck . . . . . . has to be towed away.

Insightful! Now check out these jokes that start with a funny foundation.

Why did the superhero flush the toilet?
Because it was his doody.

Why did the melon jump into the lake?

It wanted to be a watermelon.

What do you
call a vampire
that makes
pancakes?
**Count
Spatula.**

What is brown and hairy and wears
sunglasses?

A coconut on vacation.

Knock, knock.

Who's there?

Peas.

Peas who?

Peas pass the milk.

What do you call a blind dinosaur?

A do-you-think-he-saw-us.

What happened to the dog that swallowed a firefly?

It barked with de-light.

What did the judge say when the skunk walked into the courtroom?

Odor in the court!

What did one eye say to the other eye?

Don't look now, but something between us smells.

What happened to the turkey when he got into a fistfight?

He got the stuffing knocked out of him.

What do you call four bullfighters in quicksand?

Quattro sinko.

How do you fix a broken pizza?

With tomato paste.

What does a shark like to eat with peanut butter?

Jellyfish.

Why did the banana go to the doctor?
It wasn't peeling well.

Mom said I'd never be able to build a real car out of spaghetti.
You should've seen her reaction when I drove pasta.

My mother told me to take the bananas off my feet. I don't know why. They were perfectly good slippers.

What are elephants that wear tiny glass slippers?
Cinderelephants.

Why are ninja farts so dangerous?
They're silent but deadly.

How do you make a tissue dance?
Put a little boogie in it.

How did the farmer mend his pants?
With cabbage patches.

What do space cows say?
Moooo-n.

Why don't you ever hear a pterodactyl use the bathroom?
Because the p is silent.

What's the quickest way to mail a little horse?
Pony Express.

What do you call a pig that knows karate?
A pork chop.

Grab a fork, head to the next room, and try a heaping helping of pun pie!

PLAYING with WORDS:
ANOTHER ONE FIGHTS THE DUST

Zoom on in! Vinnie the Vac here, all revved up to tell you about wordplay. I'm pumped that I get to do the talking in this room today! Usually, there's this really cool cat who gives the tour, but the cat disappeared—strangely—so today it's all me. For the first time in a while, I get to do more than just collect dust.

Get it? *More than just collect dust!*
That's wordplay—creating surprise by
playing on words' double meanings, sim-
ilar sounds, spellings, or contrasts.

Did I explain that okay? Did I clean
house? I think so! I'm not like the other
vacuums. They're mostly dirtbags.

LOLA, what can you churn up for us
today?

Hey there, Vinnie.
Do you have a Band-Aid?
I just scraped my knee
falling for you.

Uh . . . that was a good use of wordplay, because *falling* has two meanings, but . . .

Are you a broom?
Because you're sweeping
me off my feet.

Yeah . . . *swept* has two meanings, too, but, first, don't ever call me a broom. And, second, we vacuums pick up on stuff, so I get what you're saying. I better roll on out of here!

Where is that cat?!

YOUR TURN!

I'm going to hang out on this page—away from that lady machine. I need to keep things upright! A vacuum can't have too many attachments.

Here are six ways you can use wordplay to make your friends laugh:

Six Ways to Be Punny and Funny

1. Homonyms: Words that sound alike and are spelled alike but have different meanings—like *"suit yourself"* and *"he wore a suit."*

Use a homonym to create a joke like this:

Why did the tomato turn red?
It saw the salad **dressing**.

2. Homophones: Words that sound alike but have different spellings and different meanings, like *pair*, *pare*, and *pear* or *to*, *too*, and *two*.

Use a homonym to create a joke like this:

What do you call a number that can't keep still?
A *roamin'* numeral.

3. Malapropisms: Words that are used in place of similar-sounding words.

There's a malapropism in the famous vacuum motto "Another one *fights* the dust!" (instead of "*bites* the dust"). Use a malapropism to create a joke like this:

I tried to catch some fog, but I *mist*.

4. Oxymorons: Words that are put together but seem like opposites, like *jumbo shrimp, modern history, pretty ugly, computer jock, definitely maybe, exact estimate, sweet sorrow, silent scream, good grief,* and *butthead.*

Oxymorons are just naturally funny. Use an oxymoron to create a joke like this:

This library is filled with such a **deafening silence**, I can't hear what you're saying.

5. Spoonerisms: A few letters that are switched change the meaning of the phrase, like: *a pack of lies/a lack of pies, take a shower/shake a tower, it's pouring with rain /it's roaring with pain.*

Use a spoonerism to create a joke like this:

He thinks he's a **smart fella**, but he's really a **fart smella**.

6. Mondegreens: A new phrasing created after something has been misheard.

Instead of singing the right words to the US national anthem, "O say can you see," you could sing, *"Jose, can you see?"* Use mondegreens like this:

My mom's always singing a song that goes, **"You fill up my senses."** I was glad I figured out the real words, because I thought she was singing, **"You fill out my *census*."**

Now, enjoy these jokes while I get back to looking for the cat. That sneaky furball really left me in the dust!

What do you call a spaceship that drips water?
A *crying* saucer.

What do you get when you cross a fish and an elephant?
Swimming *trunks*.

Why did the belt go to jail?
It *held up* a pair of pants.

Why was the ant confused?
Because all his uncles were *ants*.

What do you call a cow with no legs?
Ground beef.

Two blood cells met and fell in love.
Too bad it was all in *vein*.

Why did the scarecrow get a raise?
He was *outstanding* in his field.

What do
you call a
cow on a
trampoline?
A *milkshake*.

When is a door not a door?
When it's *ajar*.

What did the light bulb say to his wife
on Valentine's Day?
I love you *watts and watts*!

How do trees get on the internet?
They *log* in.

What do you call a fake noodle?
An *impasta*.

What do you call it when a dinosaur
crashes its car?
Tyrannosaurus *wrecks*.

What does a skeleton order for dinner?
***Spare ribs*.**

What goes *zzub, zzub, zzub*?
A *bee flying backward*.

What do you get when you cross a cow
and a duck?
***Milk and quackers*.**

Knock, knock!
Who's there?
Ketchup.
Ketchup who?
Ketchup **with me and I'll tell you!**

Why did the lion spit out the clown?
Because he *tasted funny*.

Why can't pirates learn the alphabet?
They always get lost at *c*.

What happened when nineteen and
twenty got into a fight?
Twenty *one*.

Why was the baby strawberry crying?
Because her parents were in a *jam*.

What is an astronaut's favorite key on
the keyboard?
The *space bar*.

What lies at the bottom of the ocean
and twitches?
A *nervous wreck*.

118

How do you organize a space party?
You *planet* early.

Why didn't the skeleton cross the road?
He *didn't have the guts*.

How much does a pirate pay for corn?
A *buccaneer*.

Knock, knock.
Who's there?
Norma Lee.
Norma Lee who?
***Norma Lee* I don't knock on doors, but I wanted to say hi!**

Why are graveyards noisy?
Because of all the *coffin*.

What did the mama cow say to the baby cow?
It's *pasture* bedtime.

What day of the week does a potato dread?
***Fry-day*!**

What did the policeman say to his stomach?
Freeze! You're _under a vest!_

What did one plate say to the other plate?
Dinner is _on me._

What do you call cheese that isn't yours?
**Nacho cheese.**

What did the hat say to the scarf?
You _hang around_, and I'll _go on a head._

Why was the bee's hair sticky?
Because she used a _honey-comb._

Did you hear about the race between the lettuce and the tomato?

The lettuce was *ahead*, and the tomato was trying to *ketchup*!

What did the teddy bear say when it was offered birthday cake?

No thanks, I'm *stuffed*.

What kind of underwear do reporters wear?

News *briefs*.

What do you call a three-footed aardvark?

A *Yardvark*.

What did one elevator say to the other elevator?

I think I'm *coming down* with something.

The local ice-skating rink charges a dollar an hour.

What a *cheap skate*!

I've often heard that "icy" is the easiest word to spell.
Looking at it now, *I see why*.

How do you know when a joke becomes too corny?
When it's *full groan*.

Why do Viking ships have bar codes?
So that when they get to port, they can *Scandinavian*.

What did the salad say during the fire?
***Lettuce romaine* calm.**

Where do burgers like to dance?
At the *meatball*.

Roll on off to the next room. There's more silliness ahead!

TWIZZLING:
SOCK IT TO ME!

Slide on in! I'm ready to *rock your socks off* with something I call **twizzling**.

Twizzling is taking a common saying, catchphrase, motto, or slogan and twisting it into a fab new thing. It's starting with something like "That is *so* last year" and bending it into "That is *so* 30 minutes ago" or "That is *so* back in kindergarten."

Just change up a few words and you've got a totally chill—and silly—new saying.

Or—oh my goodness!—you can take something like "Granola is the new cookie" and twizzle it into "Slimy is the new sticky" or "Fab is the new rad" or "Cotton socks are the new chicken soup"—all majorly true statements.

I'm so into this I even twizzled a name for my totally sick socks. How cool are they? Instead of "Goody Two-Shoes," I call them "Goody Two-Socks." At the end of the day, they smell like Goody Four-Socks, but I still love them! If people say my socks are stinky, I tell them, "If you can't take the feet, stay out of the yoga room." Another twizzle!

Now let's see what **LOLA** can twist up.
Sock it to me, **LOLA**!

I wish
I could twist like you!
Teach me how. I'm ready for
hard work. My motto is, "No pain,
no fast lane, gravy train,
castle in Spain."

Awesome twizzle of "No pain, no gain,"
LOLA, but you're a 98,302-ton machine!
You're really cute and you have some
great colors going on, but there's no way

you can twist like me. You can't even move. If you even tried, you'd get a twitch in your giddyup.

**I want to learn!
Every morning I want to
rise and entwine!**

No can do, girl. Sorry, but you're on cloud 19.

YOUR TURN!

Let's talk about how you can twizzle your way into more laughs. (And you should definitely take my advice, because I straight up—and twisted 'round—know what I'm talking about.)

Start with a basic catchphrase, and change up a few words. Don't change too much, though, because your squad still needs to recognize the original saying for it to be funny. Then mix in unusual off-the-grid details that fit the situation just right.

TRY THIS:

Change a few words so the catchphrase has a new meaning:

Original: You have to kiss a lot of frogs before you find a prince.
Twizzled: You have to kiss a lot of frogs before you get thrown out of a pet store.

Original: To err is human; to forgive is divine.
Twizzled: To err is human; to purr is feline.

Original: I'd walk across fire for you.
Twizzled: I'd walk across Legos for you.

Change the last word to another that rhymes with the original:

Original: You can lead a horse to water, but you can't make him drink.
Twizzled: You can lead a horse to water, but you can't make him lip-synch.

Change one word in the catchphrase to its opposite:

Original: And the plot thickens.
Twizzled: And the plot thinnens.

Take the basic structure, and change its context:

Original: You're not the sharpest tool in the shed.
Twizzled: You're not the brightest bulb in the chandelier.

Twizzled: You're not the tightest string on the guitar.

Change the wording of a catchphrase to fit the situation:

Original: Liar, liar, pants on fire.
Twizzled: Why do you call me a liar when clearly my pants are not on fire?

Original: That cost an arm and a leg.
Twizzled: That was superexpensive! I want my arm and leg back.

Get the saying wrong on purpose:

Original: You're batting a thousand.
Twizzled: You're batting a thousand and twenty-six.

Original: I'm so clumsy it's like I have two left feet.
Twizzled: I'm so clumsy it's like I have five left feet.

Add words to the end:

Original: We're not on the same page.
Twizzled: We're not on the same page. We're not even in the same book.

Original: You can't fit a square peg in a round hole.
Twizzled: You can't fit a square peg in a round hole—unless you have a chisel and a mountain of sandpaper.

Now spiral on into these jokes!

I'm so far out of the loop I'll never find my way back in, not even with Google Maps.

We're studying short stories in English. One thing I learned quickly: It's easy for an English teacher to make a short story long.

What did the horse say before he went to sleep?
Time to hit the hay.

Why did the chicken cross the road, swim in the mud, then cross the road again?
Because it was a dirty double-crosser.

My friend told me to stop being a flamingo. So I put my foot down.

I get enough exercise just pushing my luck.

What's the motto of the ghouls convention?
The morgue the merrier.

Slept like a log last night... woke up in the fireplace.

There are two kinds of people in this world: people who love the first day of school, and people who prefer dental surgery.

If you think money can't buy happiness, I have two words for you: **Deep fried.**

My horse looked sad, so I asked, "Why the long face?"

Never mind cats and dogs, it was raining chickens and ducks yesterday. Fowl weather.

What did the cat say on the phone?
Can you hear meow?

He's so cheap he can't give you the time of day.

He's a whole chicken, three biscuits, and nine brownies short of a picnic.

What did the alien say to the dandelion?
Take me to your weeder.

I ordered a chicken and an egg from Amazon. I'll let you know which comes first.

My aunt's huge parrot just died. It was a big weight off her shoulder.

What did the chimp say when his sister was having a baby?
I'll be a monkey's uncle.

A wagon full of people playing all sorts of instruments rode down my street. One of them yelled, "Quick, jump on the bandwagon."

The hospital called and said Grandma's on her last leg. Then I wondered, how many did she have?

Calendars are old-fashioned. Their days are numbered.

I tried to grab the toy away from the baby. He grabbed it back. Turns out he wasn't born yesterday.

Hey, long time, no . . .

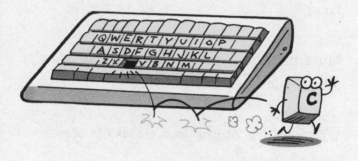

Twist and turn toward the next room for more rib-tickling fun!

FAMOUS STUFF:
EINSTEIN AND STICKY POCKETS

Don't be scared—well, maybe just a little scared. I'm Dr. Dragg, famed supervillain!

What? You've never heard of me? *Impossible!* My face is on wanted posters, bus signs, and cereal boxes across the country—the good cereal, too, not the kind that tastes like tree bark.

Come in and hold still. I need to scan your brain for sensitive information and check your pockets.

Grrrunch, crrrinkle, zzzleep.

Okay, you're safe. And harmless. And have a surprisingly sticky wad of gum in your pocket. Yuck!

I'm taking time off from being positively evil to tell you how to use famous stuff to make your friends laugh.

Referencing famous people, places, movies, and things can be funny. It's a dreadfully good way to associate your thought with something we all know and turn it into something new. Like if I say, "Sure thing, Einstein," you know I mean, "Sure thing, smart guy."

So instead of explaining stuff in a long, windbaggy kind of way, cut through the jibber-jabber and create a quick comparison to something we all understand. Don't be like that supervillain from the comics who gets himself twisted up in the blah blah blah and yada yada yada while the superhero slips away.

LOLA, blast us with a joke! I need to get back to taking over the world. And fixing my ray gun. And my villain-mobile is double-parked.

You're all over the place! What are you—Wi-Fi?

Oooh, darkly delicious, associating my menacing movements with Wi-Fi, a thing everyone knows. Shoot another joke at me, **LOLA**, and this time make it positively sinister. ***Mwah-ha-ha!***

You're firing out some spicy words. Cool down, jambalaya.

POW! You hit the mark, associating my words with a popular spicy dish. You know, **LOLA**, you'd make a great super-villain sidekick. If this place has an access ramp, I can wheel you over to the dark side.

Hold up, Darth Vader. I can't double as a supervillain. A joke machine needs her beauty sleep!

YOUR TURN!

To create your own jokes using famous stuff, check your pockets. I mean check the instructions below. *Don't check your pockets!* I didn't take anything. If you're missing something, it wasn't me!

TO CREATE JOKES USING FAMOUS STUFF:

1. **Pick a famous person, place, or thing that has a connection with your thought. Make sure it's someone, someplace, or something the person you're talking to will know.**

139

2. Zero in on the famous person, place, or thing's obvious trait—like my despicable demeanor.

3. Keep your joke short and to the point. No dreadful dribble!

4. Let the reference speak for itself, don't be a peabrain and explain it!

Got it? Good. Brainstorm and create your own famous-stuff jokes, like these:

This place is a mess. Who ate here—Wreck-It Ralph?

The 1980s called. They want their mullet back.

You're going away again? Who are you, Flat Stanley?

That rhymes. Good job, Dr. Seuss.

Ew, that bologna is as green as Shrek.

You're saying some salty stuff. Do you think you're the Atlantic Ocean or something?

Important people, sit in the front. Everyone else, over there in Siberia.

People don't do that anymore. Who are we, the Flintstones?

My hair's pretty crazy today. It looks like it was styled by a Troll doll.

Don't give me the cold shoulder—you're not Alaska.

Nice yellow shirt. Did you swipe that from Big Bird's closet?

Calm down, Kermit. We all know you like the color green.

You must be Google Maps, 'cause you have everything I'm searching for.

Now charge into these fiendish famous-stuff jokes:

What's red and goes "oh, oh, oh"?
Santa walking backward!

How did Darth Vader know what Luke got him for Christmas?
He felt his presents!

Why did Mozart sell his chicken?
Because it kept saying "Bach, Bach, Bach."

Why does the Mississippi River see so well?
Because it has five eyes!

Why did the Cyclops close his school?
Because he had only one pupil.

Why does Peter Pan always fly?
Because he can Neverland.

What do you call a cow that won't give milk?
A Milk Dud.

What do you call a droid that takes the long way around?
R2 detour.

What is Tarzan's favorite Christmas song?
Jungle Bells.

What do you call security guards at Samsung shops?
Guardians of the Galaxy.

Simba was walking slow, so I told him to Mufasa.

Why can't Mickey Mouse add?
He has only four fingers on each hand.

What car does Luke Skywalker drive?
Toy-Yoda.

What did George Washington say to his troops before they crossed the Delaware?
Get in the boat!

I named my new iPad the *Titanic*. Now, when I plug it into my laptop, it says, "The *Titanic* is syncing."

What fairy doesn't take a bath?
Stinkerbell.

What did Daisy Duck say when she bought lipstick?
Put it on my bill.

Why is Alabama the smartest state?
Because it has four As and one B.

What was the patriots' favorite food in the Revolutionary War?
Chicken Catch-a-Tory.

What tower can't eat anything?
The I Full Tower.

What did Delaware?
A New Jersey.

What's the capital of Washington?
W.

What do you call Clark Kent with
diarrhea?
Pooperman.

Now act like a NASCAR driver and peel
out of here!

MAKING JUNK UP:
A HEAPING PILE OF MUSHARONI

Slippity-dip on in here! It's time to bake up gigglicious made-up words.

Who better to mash-potato words together than a mushy brain like me? Some parts of me are as solid as a Ring Ding, and other parts are complete musharoni. And when I say "musharoni," I mean "squishy-mishy," and when I say "squishy-mishy," I mean . . . uh, what was I talking about?

Brilzilliant brain surgeons have studied me for years. They believe I'm fabtabulous at making up words because the silly-chilly section of my cerebral cortex is especially well developed.

See for yourself in this recent X-ray:

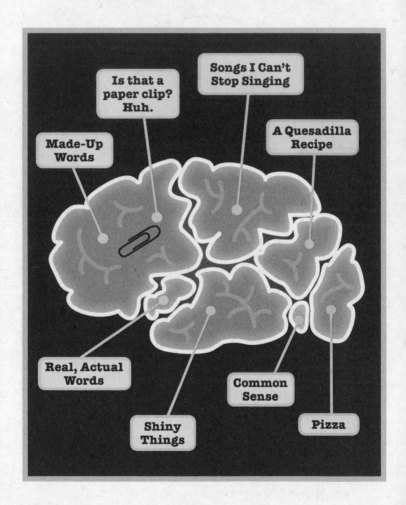

LOLA, time to noodle up a new word!

Yeaaah,
I'm not feeling very
worky today.

Worky is a marvillious made-up word!
We get its meaning zippity-quick. It
requires no thought, even for me. **LOLA**,
zap up another word!

149

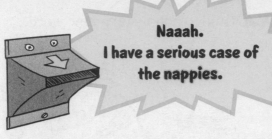

**Naaah.
I have a serious case of the nappies.**

Luckily, I know what the word **nappies** means, because I have a fictionary, which is a dictionary of flexcellent made-up words. The nappies is a dreadawful medical condition: when you have oodles to do, but you take a nap anyway. Nighty-nuzzle, **LOLA**! Happy horizontaling!

Play around mishmashing words together until you've come up with oodoley doodles of your own. Just keep this in your noggin: Your friends need to get your new word's meaning easy-peasy, just from its sound. Once you have a brand-clanking-new word, you'll wonderoo how you ever lived without it!

Ten SMASHTASTIC Ways to Make Up Words

1. Create a **portmanteau**, which, shockingly, is a real word. A portmanteau is a mash-up of two words to create a new one—like combining *bad* and *attitude* to get *baditude*.

2. Use **onomatopoeia**, which, astonishingly, is also a real word. An onomatopoeia is a word that describes its sound—like *zzeek* or *bamm* or *bloop*!

3. Put a well-known ending on a word—like *textpectation* or **Mexpectation**, *for when you're anticipating a text or Mexican food.*

4. Put a common beginning on a word—like *fabtabulous* or *fabmazing*.

5. Turn a noun into a verb, like telling your friends you're *TVing* or *home-working*, or when you want cake and you say, "**Cake me!**"

6. Create your own **acronym** or **initialism**. An acronym is an abbreviation that is pronounced like a word—such as *FOMO*, for "fear of missing out." An initialism is a group of letters that stand for a word. It's pronounced letter by letter—like *TLC*, for "tender loving care."

7. Change up a compound word, switching the second half of the word to something that rhymes with it—like changing *ringtone* to *ring-groan* or *ring-clone*. Then think of funny definitions for each word:

Ring-clone (*noun*): What results when someone copies your ringtone.

Ring-groan (*noun*): The sound you make when you hear your ringtone and don't feel like talking.

8. Make up a word for a condition—like **perkatory** to describe time spent with someone who's way too perky, or **karmageddon** for a time when you're bursting with good karma.

9. Make up a complete nonsense word that has absolutely no meaning and can be used anytime—like **jambungled** or **snockeldoo** or **gopey-dopes**:

I couldn't sleep last night, and now my head feels all **jambungled**.

10. Make up a superlong word to sound extrasmart—like *pseudophenomenous* or *gastrohyperphobish*. Use your new words in a joke:

I've been using a lot of big words lately to make myself sound more *pseudophenomenous*.

After studying diagrams of the digestive system, my stomach is starting to feel very *gastrohyperphobish*.

Zippity-dip into more spectaculous jokes:

What kind of shorts do clouds wear?
Thunderwear.

What's the funniest candy in the world?
LOL-lipop.

What do you call someone who's afraid of Santa?
Claustrophobic.

I stink at badminton. When I play, it's more like **sadminton**.

How do ghosts like their chicken?
Terror-fried.

What do cows use in their texts?
E-moo-jis.

What do you call a dog magician?
A labracadabrador.

How do rabbits travel?
By hareplane.

What time do you go to the dentist?
Tooth hurty!

What do you call a sad coffee?
A depresso.

June is over. Let's start **Julying**.

What do you get if you eat Christmas decorations?
Tinselitus.

LAUGH LAB'S
Excerpts from the
Fictionary

Alabummer—when you're sad that you have to leave Alabama.

Buttersigh—the sound you make when a pretty butterfly flits away.

Connectiwhat?—when you can't remember how to spell Connecticut.

Cookie-sludge—the goop on the bottom of a glass of milk after you've dunked cookies in it.

Couchouch—the stinging
feeling you get after
you stub your
toe on the
couch.

Feefiphobia—a fear of giants.

Germinator—a person who cleans very
aggressively.

Heapopotamus—when you're glad
you were given a heaping helping of
hippopotamus stew.

Panquake—when you quiver with joy
because you know pancakes are coming.

Spideyhopping—the frantic dance you
do after you've just seen a spider.

Unawerewolf—a werewolf who isn't
paying attention.

Wormwail—the sound you make when
you bite into an apple and find half a
worm.

I stay up every night studying the stars in an attempt to become more **astrogalatical**...and then it dawns on me.

I studied for hours. Now I'm going to **lazilangorous** the afternoon away.

Because of your **SPAM** (**seriously poor attitude, man**), I'm not calling you.

Skeedoodle to the next room. More hooting and katootling await!

GETTING IT WRONG:
WORKING 25/7

Hello? Hello?!

What a pickle! My cell phone's not working, and I need to call my grandson. He wants to give me an app, but I'm on a diet.

Hmm. I can't even contact him on Snapcat or Bookface, because I accidentally deleted the internet.

Oh dear. We better move on. The scientists here want me to show you a very fancy formula about how you can make your friends laugh by getting simple facts wrong. Now where is it? It has lots of letters and numbers and slanted lines—it's even on graph paper. Oh, here it is!

My word. That's not a scientific formula. That's a recipe for lasagna. Maybe . . .

Good grief! That's a map of the zoo.

Well, I'll just tell you what the nice scientists told me. It's funny when you get something wrong on purpose. It's as if I say, "I'm not going. N-O, which spells 'I'll meet you there.'" It's funny because we know that's not what N-O spells.

Okay, **LOLA**, here are some treats. Cook up a joke!

Your treats are so yummy!
I can sum you up in one word:
BEST COOK ON THE PLANET!

WHOOZY-
WHATZY
pat. pending

Well, doesn't that take the cheesecake! That was a lot more than one word. Isn't **LOLA** a doozie? What's the matter, you don't recognize the word *doozie*? It's ancient Greek for "horsefeathers." At least I think it is . . .

Now it's time to fiddle up your own wrongs.

Ten Tremendous Ways to Get It Wrong

1. **Get well-known facts wrong:**

I'm really trying to solve the problem. My brain is working 25/7.

This is an emergency! Quick, someone call 1-1-6!

On our class trip to Washington, DC, we'll see the Jefferson Memorial, the Washington Monument, and the Eiffel Tower.

2. Mix things up from the past and present:

Lucky for us, the Romans invented the iPad, the electric blanket, and salsa dancing, because without those things we'd still be in the Dark Ages.

If you don't pay extra for shipping, they send it by Pony Express.

I love quotes from the past. My favorite is Thomas Jefferson's famous line: **"Hey, dude, can you dig it?"**

3. Get numbers wrong:

On a scale of 1 to 10, you're an 11.

Brother: I'm going to ask Mom if I can spend all day at the arcade. What do you think she'll say?
You: There's a 50 percent chance she'll say, "No," a 70 percent chance she'll say, "No way," and a 110 percent chance she'll say, "Get upstairs and clean your room."

Four out of three people find fractions difficult.

There are three types of people in this world: those who can count and those who can't.

4. Get time wrong:

This milk tastes old. The "sell-by" date is 1719, so I think it's expired.

Why are you worried? I'll spend an hour on the essay, an hour on history, and a half hour on math. I'll be done in five minutes.

That old Mustang is so cool. And fast. It took only 10 minutes to drive it from the 1960s to my driveway.

5. Get geography wrong:

I want to move to a state with a beautiful oceanfront, like Kansas.

Friend: That's a great dress. Is it from Europe?

You: No, France.

6. Mix up words so the details are wrong:

You're saying we can't stand downwind from him because he likes to **tart**?

His speech was one big confusing word coleslaw.

7. Make up a fact:

Friend: Don't worry; you have enough battery.

You: I don't know. Cell phones drain 65 percent faster when you're using them for homework.

This video game isn't based on computer code. There are some serious little dudes in my monitor who run around and bang one another over their heads.

Mars rovers don't run on gas. They run on hair gel and stale doughnuts.

8. **Exaggerate something that's kind of true:**

Yowza! That's a complicated equation. We need a 130-year-old to figure it out.

In 10 years, the hardest thing to do will be to find a password that's not taken.

Thunder is the sound caused by lightning. It means there's been a sudden increase in temperature, the air has expanded rapidly, and you'd better get inside before you're barbecued like a side of ribs.

166

9. Get a random thing wrong:

A poncho is a giant piece of plastic you wear in the rain. **It's the poor, nerdy cousin of the cape.**

You: Cowabunga!
Friend: Stop quoting him.
You: Why? I love Shakespeare.

Anika is an extremely positive person. **There's nothing she can't put lip gloss on.**

10.

What's #10 doing here? There is no #10.

Oh dear, I must have counted nine techniques and my tuna sandwich.

Enjoy these jokes while I figure out the difference between these things.

I feel like I've been to this restaurant before.
Are you having déjà vu?
No, I'm having the chicken.

Mom: Time to pack for vacation.
Daughter: Vacation?
Mom: It's short for "vacay."

I give up. I've spent hours trying to teach my brother to multiply and he still thinks 4 x 5 = banana.

A recent scientific study showed that out of 2,293,618,367 people, 94 percent are too lazy to actually read that number.

This store is awesome; it's open nine days a week!

You must be the square root of –1, because you're too beautiful to be real.

Knock, knock.

Who's there?

Nobel.

Nobel who?

No bell, that's why I knocked!

Why is England the wettest country?
Because the queen has reigned there for years.

The early days of history were called the Dark Ages because there were so many knights.

So when you said, "Get up early," did you mean 1986?

Go to my locker and take out my wallet. There's a lot of money in there that you can have to spend on anything you want. Here's my locker combination:

$$5 \text{ right}, \quad \sqrt{486} \text{ left}, \quad \frac{13.1}{\pi} \text{ right}$$

Abraham Lincoln walked eight miles to school every day. Apparently, he missed the bus a lot.

Teacher: Where is the English Channel?
Student: I don't know, my TV doesn't pick it up.

What's the shortest month?
May, it only has three letters.

Mom bought a head of lettuce. I have no idea what she did with the body.

Always check your spelling. That's something my feather taught me.

I'm not full of denial, I've never even been on that river in Egypt.

I don't know why I need to go to school; I already know everything. School should clothes for good, totally shirt down.

I'm not sorry I spent my life savings on golden retrievers. They retrieve gold, right?

The propeller is just a big fan in the front of the plane that keeps the pilot cool.
It stopped working.
We'll be okay, but the pilot may start sweating.

I saw a book on how to solve 50 percent of your problems. I bought 2 copies.

The credit card company keeps calling to say my payment is outstanding. Why are they complimenting me? I never paid them.

My sister watched an ant pick up a candy wrapper that was 10 times its body weight. She said, "Can you imagine being that strong?" I picked up the wrapper and said, "Yes."

My teacher asked if I was responsible. I said yes. Whenever something goes wrong, everyone says I'm responsible.

Hurry off to the next room. I just got a call on my email, and I need to answer it before it stops ringing.

JUMP INTO THE JOKE:
DRIBBLE AND SCRIBBLE

Hey, come in and find the remote for me. I'm staring at videos of waterskiing cats because there's no way I'm getting off the couch. I don't feel like doing anything.

I don't even feel like finishing this sentence.

I love being funny,
but there's no way I'm creating
my own joke. Too much work. Instead,
I take an existing joke and jump into it.

I tell the joke as if it's a story that happened to me. By the time I get to the punch line, my friend has figured out that it's a joke.* Works every time. It's as easy as saying "K," because saying "okay" takes too much energy.

I've blabbed enough. **LOLA**, do your thing. Spit out a classic joke I can jump— or fall—into, since there's no way I'm jumping.

WHOOZY-WHATZY
pat. pending

Sure, but you need to clean up! Green fuzz is growing on your chocolate milk, there's a pile of old pancakes on my throttle booster, and there's a ketchup stain on the hamster!

---

* Make sure you're starting with a classic joke, or creating your own spin on another's joke. Directly ripping off a line from someone else is not cool.

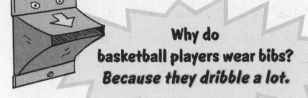

Here goes...

Why do basketball players wear bibs? Because they dribble a lot.

Golden. Now, when you're talking to a friend, put yourself in the joke. Start by setting the scene:

You: I went to a basketball game with my dad last night.
Friend: How was it?
You: Weird. All the players wore bibs.
Friend: What?!
You: They have to. They dribble a lot.

Easy, right? So if you're feeling chill, put your joke-making buzz into power-save mode and jump (or fall) into an existing joke.

Since you're using existing jokes in this room, and since I'm overdue for my nap, it's a good time for you to work

176

on delivery. I don't mean pizza delivery (although that sounds awesome—please order me one); I mean how to tell a joke.

Should you use silly body movements? A screwy face? Googly eyes? A twisted mouth? Sound effects, like a zombie groan? Your decision.

So now it's all you. Read this stuff and practice. Oh, and let me know when you find the remote.

Ten Tip-Top Tactics for Telling a Joke

1. Start with a joke you like, one that fits your personality.

2. Add details from your life or other specifics to make it your own.

3. Listen to how comics incorporate funny voices, body movements, and facial expressions. Watch how they vary the tone or inflection of their voice at key points.

4. Practice telling the joke in a mirror or to a close friend. Once you feel confident, move to a small group of friends.

5. Pick the right time and place to tell your joke, one where everyone is relaxed and ready to listen.

6. Be cool during the setup and buildup. Don't give away that the punch line is coming.

7. Pause before the punch line. You can emphasize the pause by shrugging, shaking your head, or making some type of body movement.

8. Deliver the last words with confidence, in an exaggerated, funny way.

9. Don't laugh at your own joke. If your friends don't laugh, don't push it. Just move to another topic.

10. If someone doesn't "get" your joke, don't take it personally. Different people laugh at different things. Keep experimenting with new jokes and varied audiences.

Laze into these jokes. You can laugh without even getting off the couch.

Existing Joke

Why don't lobsters share?

Because they're shellfish.

☛ **YOUR JOKE**

You: My mom made lobsters last night. They tasted good, but they had terrible personalities.

Friend: What?

You: They're so shellfish.

Existing Joke

Why did the bike fall over?

It was two tired.

☛ **YOUR JOKE**

You: I love my new bike. Too bad it keeps falling over.

Friend: Why's that?

You: It's two tired.

Existing Joke

Why was the baseball game windy?

There were too many fans.

 YOUR JOKE

I went to the game with my dad last night.

It was a great game, except it was really windy.

Too many fans.

Existing Joke

Why did the chicken cross the road?

It thought it was an egg-cellent idea.

 YOUR JOKE

You: Yesterday I actually saw a chicken cross Belmont Street.

Friend: No way!

You: I couldn't believe it, either. Apparently, it thought it was an egg-cellent idea.

Existing Joke

Why did the cookie go to the doctor?

He was feeling crummy.

☞ YOUR JOKE

You: I went to the doctor's yesterday. When I got there, it was so weird. There were cookies everywhere.

Friend: Why?

You: I guess they were feeling crummy.

Existing Joke

Did you know there's a glass of milk in every chocolate bar?

It's not the milk that bothers me, it's the glass.

☞ **YOUR JOKE**

You: I read there's a glass of milk in every chocolate bar.

Friend: Really?

You: Yeah, the milk is cool. It's the glass that bothers me.

Existing Joke

Today I met the person who invented "zero." I told her, "Thanks for nothing."

☞ **YOUR JOKE**

You: There was a lady at the library last night who was walking around telling everyone she invented "zero."

Friend: Did you talk to her?

You: Yeah, I said, "Thanks for nothing."

Existing Joke

What word is always spelled wrong in the dictionary?

Wrong!

 YOUR JOKE

You: I was looking up our spelling words last night, and I found a word in the dictionary that was spelled wrong.

Friend: Really? What word?

You: Wrong.

Existing Joke

The universe finally answered my request to win the lottery. The answer was no.

 YOUR JOKE

You: Great news! The universe finally answered me when I asked to win the lottery.

Friend: No way!

You: Yes! Too bad the answer was no.

Existing Joke

Why did the cow cross the street?

To go to the mooovies!

YOUR JOKE

You: Yesterday I saw a cow cross Main Street.

Friend: Really?

You: Yeah, he was on his way to the mooovies.

Existing Joke

The world's most famous tongue twister champion was just arrested. I bet he gets a long sentence.

YOUR JOKE

You: Did you hear the world's most famous tongue twister champion was arrested?

Friend: No.

You: Yeah. Worst part is, he's getting a long sentence.

Existing Joke

My dad just finished building a car engine from a washing machine. Later, he's going to take it for a spin.

 YOUR JOKE

You: My dad's amazing. He built a car engine from a washing machine.

Friend: Really?

You: Yeah, later he's going to take it for a spin.

Existing Joke

My grandfather kept warning everyone that the *Titanic* would sink. They wouldn't listen to him, but they did kick him out of the theater.

 YOUR JOKE

You: My grandfather was a smart guy. He kept warning everyone that the *Titanic* would sink.

Friend: Really?

You: Yeah, sadly no one would listen. Then they kicked him out of the theater.

Existing Joke

Did you hear about the man who had his whole left side cut off?

He's all right now.

☛ **YOUR JOKE**

You: I saw on the news last night that a man in our town had his whole left side cut off.

Friend: How does someone live like that?

You: I don't know, but he's all right now.

Existing Joke

What is the oldest animal?

A zebra. It's still black and white.

☛ **YOUR JOKE**

You: I was watching the Discovery Channel yesterday, and they said the oldest animal in the world is the zebra.

Friend: No, it's not.

You: Yes, it is. It's still black and white.

Existing Joke

Q: What do Alexander the Great and Kermit the Frog have in common?

A: The same middle name.

YOUR JOKE

You: I spent the weekend writing a paper about what Alexander the Great and Kermit the Frog have in common.

Friend: What do they have in common?

You: Same middle name. It was a short paper.

Existing Joke

Can you call me an Uber?

You're an Uber.

YOUR JOKE

You: Even though I'm only 10, my dad asked me to call him an Uber.

Friend: You knew how to do that?

You: It was easy. I just said, "Okay, Dad, you're an Uber."

Existing Joke

Teacher: Are you sleeping in my class?

Student: No, but I could if you were a little quieter.

☞ YOUR JOKE

You: Can you believe Mrs. Rosen asked me if I was sleeping in class?

Friend: What did you say?

You: I told her I wasn't, but I could if she were quieter.

Existing Joke

I asked the librarian if she could help me this afternoon. She said no, she's booked.

☞ YOUR JOKE

You: I really wish the librarian could help me, but she can't.

Friend: Why not?

You: She's booked.

Existing Joke

Last night I saw nickels and dimes raining from the sky. I didn't worry; I knew it was just climate change.

☞ YOUR JOKE

You: You're not going to believe this. Last night I saw nickels and dimes raining from the sky.

Friend: Whoa!

You: I wasn't worried. I knew it was just climate change.

Now, either find my remote, change the channel, or beat it to the next room.

ONE BIG JELLY ROLL:
POPCORN, COOKIES, AND SUCCESS!

You did it! You made it through all the rooms in the Laugh Lab! Give yourself a hand. Well, give yourself two—and put them together in a clapping motion.

Can you smell that?

Sniff! Snuff! Phumpf!

That's the smell of success. Okay, maybe it's the smell of popcorn from the last room and Agnes's cookies, but also success!

Before Mr. Squishy and I shuffle off to bed, there's one last thing you should know. To create a *really* funny joke, try combining several techniques. Use surprise, contrast, exaggeration—as many as you can—and mix them into one big sticky jelly roll to create a humdilly of a line.

LOLA, show us how it's done!

WHOOZY-
WHATZY
pat. pending

CERTIFICATE of COMPLETION

First, a new
rule for the Laugh Lab:
Dr. Crankshaw must wear his
antisnoring mask when he sleeps.
At night, the Laugh Lab
sounds like a swamp of
dying frogs.

Comparison!
Contrast! Specifics!
Exaggeration!

No, you should wear the earplugs
I made for you! Those earplugs were
scientifically formulated out of
thermodynamic cotton balls, cotton rags,
and cotton dust. I even
threw in cotton candy!

Making junk up!
Contrast! Specifics!
Wordplay!

I tried, but even with
earplugs, I still hear a gritty rumble,
like an army of ants marching toward
a melted Snickers bar.

Comparison!
Specifics! Exaggeration!
Famous stuff!

Cool down, hot sauce!
We just want one last joke.

Contrast!
Comparison!

I can't process when you're wearing those pj's! They're a crime against fashion. Somehow they say lumberjack, kindergartner, and waffles all at the same time.

Funny foundation! Buildup and timing! Exaggeration! Specifics!

That does it! Time to push your buttons. And when I say "buttons," I mean "the mute button"!

MUTE

M.U.T.E.
(More Unbelievable Tantalizing Excitement!)

Holy hotcakes! That's not the *mute button*, that's the *M.U.T.E. button*! **OH NO!**

Wordplay!

Oh yes!!

Why didn't the skeleton
go to the dance?

Wordplay!
Being literal!

It had no body to go with.

Which king loved
fractions?

Wordplay!
Getting it wrong!
Making junk up!
Famous stuff!

Henry the One-Eighth.

Knock, knock!
Who's there?
Spell.
Spell who?
W-H-O.

Buildup
and timing!
Getting it wrong!
Being literal!

195

Why didn't Dracula have friends?

He was a pain in the neck!

Famous stuff! Twizzling! Word play!

How do you make a lemon drop?

Just let it fall.

Wordplay! Being literal!

How does a monster begin a bedtime story?

Once upon a slime.

Funny foundation! Twizzling! Wordplay!

What bus crossed the ocean?

Colum-bus!

Famous stuff! Wordplay!

Did you like the restaurant on the moon?

The food was good, but there was no atmosphere.

Being literal! Wordplay!

Knock, knock.
Who's there?
Ice cream.
Ice cream who?
I scream if you don't let us in!

Buildup and timing! Wordplay!

196

Now that you're a specialist in silliness, let's do something that's more fun than jumping on Bubble Wrap! Why are these jokes funny? Name the technique(s) each joke uses—in addition to surprise, since all jokes use surprise.

Answers are below.

This Black Forest cake is awful. It tastes like there are chunks of actual forest in it.

Exaggeration, comparison, being literal, and wordplay.

I used to dislike math, and then I realized decimals have a point.

Being literal and wordplay.

Someone dislikes math? **LOLA** and Dr. Crankshaw, march straight to the time-out corner! People not liking math is as nutty as a monkey with a kazoo.

Specifics, exaggeration, comparison, and funny foundation.

LOLA made the joke, not me! I'm not going to time-out again. That corner is dark and smells like the art room on papier-mâché day.

Specifics, comparison, buildup and timing, and exaggeration.

Hey, dude, calm down. You're steaming. And turning green. You're like steamed broccoli, only taller.

Comparison, contrast, exaggeration, and buildup and timing.

199

Did someone say broccoli? I'm hungry, and I love veggies. They're *my cup of glee* !

Buildup and timing, twizzling, and wordplay.

We're having a serious conversation here! Don't interrupt with your kooky, rooty-tooty. twizzle-drizzle.

Contrast and making junk up.

200

I'm not kooky. I'm happy with a twist.

Specifics and wordplay.

Did someone say "twist"? I've been meaning to send out a twist on that thing called Twister. Or Twipper? Or Glitter?

Buildup and timing, getting it wrong, and famous stuff.

203

Dent?
Let me at it!
I'll hammer out that
dent and buff it, fill it,
stitch it, rewire the
chassis, and stuff it
with so much kitten fur
it'll be as soft as a
bouncy castle.

Exaggeration,
specifics, and
comparison.

After that,
fix the eyeballs on
that ridiculous painting.
Tie those bouncing goo
balls on with a bungee
cord if you have to. There's
so much eyeball slime
on the floor I could
ski from one end of
the Laugh Lab
to the other.

Funny
foundation, buildup and
timing, exaggeration,
and specifics.

205

This is getting
a bit sticky.

Understatement
and wordplay.

I'll call for help. Step aside—I know which button to press.

Agnes hasn't gotten it wrong yet, but it's funny because we know she will.

This button calls my friend Anni. I think her last name is Hilation. She has a giant purse and isn't afraid to whack someone over the head with it.

Getting it wrong.

TOTAL ANNIHILATION

WATCH OUT! LOLA'S GONNA BLOW!

I hate spelling errors. If I mix up two letters, my whole post is urined.

Getting it wrong!

You: I was born a pessimist.
Friend: That's impossible.
You: No, it's not. My blood type is B negative.

Getting it wrong! Wordplay! Buildup and timing!

My doctor told me I'm color-blind. Whoa, that really came out of the orange.

Twizzling! Getting it wrong!

I was helping sell hot dogs at the football game but was asked to leave when I put my hair in a bun.

Wordplay! Contrast!

My friends don't want to hang out with me anymore because they say all I do is talk about astronomy. I don't get it. What planet are they on?

Buildup and timing! Twizzling!

It was so cold I chipped my tooth on soup.

Exaggeration! Contrast!

A lion walked into a diner and said to the waitress, "I'll have . . ." He thought about it and then said, "a juicy steak." The waitress said, "Sure, but why the long pause?"

Funny foundation! Wordplay! Buildup and timing!

We have to buy my brother three socks at a time. He just grew another foot.

Funny foundation! Being literal! Wordplay!

I called in sick to the restaurant every day last week.

Did they say "hope you feel better"?

No, they said, "You don't work here, why are you calling?"

Getting it wrong! Contrast! Building and timing!

Why don't ants get sick?

Because they have little anty bodies.

Wordplay! Funny foundation!

My best friend keeps yelling at me that I ruined her birthday.

I don't know why. I didn't even know it was her birthday.

Understatement! Building and timing!

I broke one of my fingers playing baseball. But on the other hand, everything is okay.

Understatement! Wordplay! Buildup and timing!

What do you call an elephant that doesn't matter?

Irrelephant.

Making junk up! Wordplay!

210

I was riding a horse at full speed, and a giraffe and lion were chasing me.
What did you do?
Jumped off the carousel.

Understatement!
Contrast! Buildup
and timing!

The number of people who say "boo!" on Halloween has risen 95 percent in the past year.
That's a frightening statistic.

Making junk up!
Exaggeration! Buildup
and timing! Wordplay!
Being literal!

The recipe said, "When the cookies are done, chill in the fridge for an hour."

Being literal!
Wordplay! Getting
it wrong!

The elevator's creepy.
It creaks, moans,
and yells, "You're
going down!"

Being literal!
Exaggeration! Buildup
and timing!

**The doctor tells me my voice box
is damaged. I may never speak again.
I can't tell
you how
upset I am.**

Being literal!
Buildup and timing!
Understatement!
Wordplay!

This dress makes me look like
I'm all wound up in
popped Bubble Wrap.

Specifics!
Comparison!
Exaggeration!

What do you call a
penguin in the desert?
Lost!

Contrast!
Funny foundation!
Being literal!

Knock, knock.
Who's there?
Ida.
Ida who?
No, it's Idaho.

Famous stuff! Buildup and timing! Wordplay!

Did you see the news? Three cliff walkers have fallen to their death.
Really? They all had the same name?

Understatement! Getting it wrong! Wordplay!

I bought a new pair of shoes with memory foam insoles. No more forgetting why I walked into the kitchen.

Getting it wrong! Contrast! Wordplay! Being literal!

What did one raindrop say to another?
Two's company; three's a cloud.

Funny foundation! Twizzling! Wordplay!

What do you call someone who can't fart in public?
A private tooter.

Funny foundation! Wordplay!

These jokes are so cheesy
I could dip my
nachos in them!

Exaggeration!
Wordplay!

Why can't you trust atoms?
They make up
everything.

Being literal!
Wordplay!

Is that
true?

I should
know, I wrote this
entire book.

By myself.
In an hour.

214

ACKNOWLEDGMENTS

The Laugh Lab would like to thank everyone and everything that helped make this book possible.

First, we'd like to thank cheese curls and apple juice, which kept everyone going through the long nights it took to create this book.

Next, we'd like to thank paper and ink. Without ink, this book would be, well, blank. Without paper, this book would just be a handful of ink, or—uh, we don't really know what it would be, but it wouldn't be good and it would probably stain your fingers.

Finally, we'd like to thank words. Words, you did a great job of coming together in just the right order to make us think, smile, and laugh. We couldn't end this book without a shout-out to our favorite words, which we depend on every day to express our feelings, communicate our thoughts, and fill big empty silences, like the awkward one that comes after you dribble meatballs on your shirt.

Dear **Yowza**,
Thank you for being there for us all those times we weren't sure what to say. You're a powerful punch stuffed into five letters.

Dear **LOL**,
Thank you for making our sentences cheerier—even the ones that barely make sense.

Dear **Whoa**,
Thank you for being so obscure. You fit everywhere.

Dear **Dude**,
What can we say? You're our favorite. Even though you're supposed to mean "human male," we use you to express every thought under the sun just by changing our tone. Thanks, bestie!

Dear **The End**,
Thanks for being the guy who kicks people out when it's all over.
(Some people can't take a hint.)

THE END